About the author

Mrs Gaskell was born in 1810
and died in 1865.
She wrote about ordinary people,
and the hardship of their lives.

About the story

The story is set in wild mountainous country
in the North of England

The story-teller is a young man
who tells us about his half brother **Gregory**,
their **mother** and her second husband,
William Preston,
and their **Aunt Fanny**,
who brought them up.

Mrs Gaskell's

The Half Brothers

Pub

A MEMBER OF THE HODDER HEADLINE GROUP

Acknowledgements
Cover: Matthew Williams
Illustrations: Jim Eldridge
Photograph of Mrs Gaskell © The Hulton Getty Picture Collection Limited

Orders: please contact Bookpoint Ltd, 39 Milton Park, Abingdon, Oxon OX14 4TD. Telephone: (44) 01235 400414, Fax: (44) 01235 400454. Lines are open from 9.00–6.00, Monday to Saturday, with a 24 hour message answering service. Email address: orders@bookpoint.co.uk

British Library Cataloguing in Publication Data
A catalogue record for this title is available from The British Library

ISBN 0 340 74306 9

First published 1999
Impression number 10 9 8 7 6 5 4 3 2
Year   2005 2004 2003 2002 2001 2000 1999

Typeset by Fakenham Photosetting Ltd, Fakenham, Norfolk.
Printed in Great Britain for Hodder & Stoughton Educational, a division of Hodder Headline Plc, 338 Euston Road, London NW1 3BH by Redwood Books, Trowbridge, Wiltshire.

My mother was twice married.
She never spoke of her first husband.
I believe she was scarcely seventeen
when she was married to him,
and he was barely one and twenty.

They were very poor,
and he fell into ill health,
and died of consumption.
They were married three years,
and my mother was a young widow
of twenty.

My aunt told me she did not cry,
even though she was expecting a child.
My aunt, Aunt Fanny,
would have been thankful
if she had cried,
but she was dry-eyed before,
during, and after the funeral.

She was like this
until after Gregory was born.
And somehow his coming
seemed to loosen the tears,
and she cried day and night,
night and day,
till my aunt would gladly
have stopped her, if she knew how.

But my mother told her to let her alone,
and not to worry,
for every drop she shed
eased her brain,
which had been in a terrible state
because she could not cry.

She seemed after that to think
of nothing but her new little baby.
She hardly seemed to remember
her husband who lay dead
in the churchyard.

At least so my Aunt Fanny said,
but she was a great talker,
and my mother was very silent
by nature.
I think Aunt Fanny was mistaken
in believing my mother
never thought of her husband
just because she never spoke of him.

Aunt Fanny was older than my mother,
and had a way of treating her
like a child.
But, for all that,
she was a kind, warm-hearted creature,
who thought more of her sister's welfare
than she did her own.
It was on her money that they lived,
and on what they could earn by sewing.

One day, as the sisters
were sitting together,
Aunt Fanny working,
my mother hushing Gregory to sleep,
William Preston, who later became
my father, came in.

welfare – health
and well-being

bachelor –
unmarried man

He was thought to be an old bachelor.
I suppose he was long past forty.
He was one of the richest
farmers thereabouts,
and had known my grandfather well.

He sat down,
and my Aunt Fanny talked,
and he listened and looked at my mother.
But he said very little,
either on that visit,
or on many others that he made
before he spoke out.

One Sunday, however,
my Aunt Fanny stayed away from church,
and took care of the child.
My mother went alone.

When she came back,
she ran straight upstairs,
without going into the kitchen
to look at Gregory or speak any word
to her sister.
Aunt Fanny heard her cry
as if her heart was breaking.

Aunt Fanny went up,
but the door was bolted.
Aunt Fanny shouted at her,
and told her to open it.
At last she did.
She threw herself on my aunt's neck,
and told her that William Preston
had asked her to marry him,
and had promised to take good charge
of her boy,
and that she had agreed.

Aunt Fanny was a good deal shocked;
William Preston was too old.
But then there was much to be said
on the other side –
if she was married to William Preston
my mother would never want
for anything,
and there would be a steady,
decent man to look after her.

So, by and by,
Aunt Fanny seemed to take
a brighter view of the marriage
than did my mother herself.
My mother hardly ever looked up,
and never smiled after the day
she had promised William Preston
to be his wife.

This shows how
unhappy she was.
She shared her
unhappiness with
Gregory, but he of
course was too
young to understand.

But much as she had
loved Gregory before,
she seemed to love him more now.
She was continually talking to him
when they were alone,
though he was far too young
to understand her moaning words
or give her any comfort.

At last William Preston and she
were wed, and she went to be
mistress of a well-stocked house.

mistress of a well-
stocked house
– in charge of a
rich house

I believe she did all that she could
to please my father.
But she did not love him,
and he soon found that out.
She loved Gregory,
and she did not love him.

Perhaps love would have come in time,
if he had been patient enough to wait.
But it just turned him sour
to see how much her eye brightened
at the sight of the little child,
while for him who had given her so much,
she had only gentle words
as cold as ice.

He took a dislike to Gregory –
he was so jealous of the ready love
that always gushed out
like a spring of fresh water
when he came near.
He wanted her to love him more,
and perhaps that was all well and good,
but he wanted her to love her child less,
and that was an evil wish.

This didn't change, not even
when another child was expected.

One day he gave way to his temper,
and cursed and swore at Gregory,
who had got into some mischief
as children will.
My mother made some excuse for him.

My father said it was hard
to have to keep another man's child,
and she should be of the same mind
as him.

She should always
agree with him.

And so from little they got to more,
and the end of it was, that my mother
took to her bed before her time,
and I was born that very day.

One thing led to
another.

before her time –
the baby wasn't
due yet

My father was glad and proud,
and sorry, all in a breath.
He was glad and proud
that a son was born to him,
and sorry for his poor wife's state,
and to think how his angry words
had brought it on.
But he was more angry than sorry –
he blamed it all on Gregory,
and began to have a grudge against him.

all in a breath –
all at the same time

He had another grudge against him
before long.

My mother began to sink
the day after I was born.
My father sent for doctors,

He would have
turned his blood
into gold coins
for her.

and would have coined his heart's blood
into gold to save her,
if that could have been,
but it could not.

My Aunt Fanny used to say sometimes,
that she thought my mother
did not wish to live,
and so just let herself die away
without trying to take hold on life.

request – wish

Her last request was to have Gregory
laid in her bed by my side,
and then she made him
take hold of my little hand.

My father came in
while she was looking at us so.
When he bent tenderly over her
to ask her how she felt now,
she looked up in his face and smiled,
almost her first smile at him,
and such a sweet smile!

In an hour she was dead.

Aunt Fanny came to live with us.
It was the best thing that could be done.
So she had charge of me from my birth,
and for a time I was very weak.
She was always beside me,
night and day watching over me.

My father was nearly as anxious as her.
He needed something to love,

and he took to me, I fancy,
as he had taken to no human being before.

I loved him back again right heartily.
I loved all around me, I believe,
for everybody was kind to me.
After a time I lost my weakliness,
and became a bonny, strong-looking lad.
Everyone noticed me when my father
took me with him into town.

Gregory was three years older than me.
Aunt Fanny was always kind to him

in deed and in action,
but she did not often think about him.
My father never got over
his dislike for him.
He thought he was the cause
of my mother's death.

ungainly – clumsy
marring – spoiling

scolding – telling off

Gregory was awkward and ungainly,
marring whatever he meddled in,
and he got many a hard word
and sharp scolding
from the people on the farm.

I am ashamed to say –
my heart is sore to think –
that I fell into the same way,

slighted – insulted

and slighted my poor orphan
step-brother.
I sometimes repeated the cruel words
I had heard others use about him,
without fully understanding
their meaning.
Whether he did or not, I cannot tell.
I am afraid he did.

He used to turn silent and quiet –

sullen – gloomy or
sour

sullen and sulky my father thought it,
stupid, Aunt Fanny used to call it.

But everyone said
he was stupid and dull,
and this stupidity and dullness
grew upon him.
He would sit without speaking a word,
sometimes for hours.

Then my father would bid him rise
and do some work about the farm.
And he would take three or four tellings
before he would go.

When we were sent to school,
it was all the same.
He could never be made
to remember his lessons.
The schoolmaster grew weary

flogging – beating

of scolding and flogging,
and at last told my father
just to take him away,
and set him on some farm work

above him –
too difficult for him

that might not be above him.

I think he was more gloomy and stupid
than ever after this.
Yet he was not a cross lad –
he was patient and good-natured,
and would try to do a kind turn
for anyone,
even if they had been scolding

cuffing – slapping

or cuffing him not a minute before.

He became a shepherd,
and spent his days on the Fells,
wrapped in his shepherd's cloak,
with his dog Lassie beside him.

the Fells –
high hills
covered with moors

One winter-time
when I was about sixteen,
and Gregory nineteen,
my father sent me on an errand
to a place that was about
seven miles distant by road,
but only about four by the Fells.
He told me to return by the road,
because the evenings closed in early,
and were often thick and misty.
Besides, snow was expected before long.

errand – job

I soon got to my journey's end,
and did my errand an hour sooner
than I expected.

shades – shadows

I decided to come back over the Fells,
just as the first shades of evening
began to fall.
It looked dark and gloomy enough,
but everything was so still
that I thought I should have
plenty of time to get home
before the snow came.

Off I set at a pretty quick pace.
But night came on quicker.

I took what seemed to be the right road,
but it was wrong.
It led me to some wild boggy moor,
that was so silent and lonely
it seemed no-one had ever
set foot there.

I tried to shout,
but my voice came husky and short.
Suddenly the air was filled thick
with dusky flakes.
My face and hands were wet with snow.
I lost every idea of the direction
from which I had come, so that
I could not even retrace my steps.

retrace my steps –
go back

The snow hemmed me in,
thicker, thicker,
with a darkness that might be felt.
The boggy soil on which I stood

quaked – shook

quaked under me if I remained long
in one place,
and yet I dared not move far.

hardiness – courage

All my youthful hardiness
seemed to leave me at once.

I was on the point of crying,
and to save myself, I shouted –
terrible, wild shouts for bare life.
No answering sound came

The echoes are
unfeeling because
they bring no
comfort to him.

but the unfeeling echoes.

Only the noiseless,
pitiless snow kept falling
thicker, thicker – faster, faster!

I was growing numb and sleepy.
I tried to move about,
but I dared not go far,
for fear of the many cliffs on the Fells.

I gathered up my strength,
and called out once more,
a long, despairing, wailing cry,
to which I had no hope
of hearing any answer.

To my surprise, I heard a bark.
Was it Lassie's bark –
my brother's collie?

Yes! there again! It was Lassie's bark!
Now or never!
I lifted up my voice and shouted
'Lassie! Lassie!
For God's sake, Lassie!'
Another moment,
and the great white-faced Lassie
was curving and gambolling with delight
round my feet and legs.

gambolling –
playing and
skipping

I cried with gladness,
as I stooped down and patted her.
I knew that help was at hand.
A grey figure came out of the darkness.
It was Gregory wrapped in his cloak.

'Oh, Gregory!' I said,
and fell upon his neck,
unable to speak another word.

He never spoke much,
and made no answer for some little time.
Then he told me we must move,
we must walk for dear life –
we must find our road home, if possible,
but we must move
or we should be frozen to death.

'Don't you know the way home?' I asked.

'I thought I did when I set out,
but I am doubtful now.
The snow blinds me, and I am afraid
that in moving about just now,
I have lost the right way homewards.'

We set off.
He was more guided by Lassie
and the way she took than anything else,
trusting to her instinct.
It was too dark to see far before us,
but he called her back continually,
and noted from where she came,
shaped – pointed   and shaped our steps accordingly.

But this slow progress
scarcely kept my blood from freezing.
Every bone, every fibre in my body
seemed first to ache, then to swell,
and then to turn numb
with the intense cold.

My brother bore it better than me,
from having been more out
upon the hills.
He did not speak, except to call Lassie.

I tried to be brave, and not complain,
but now I felt the deadly fatal sleep
stealing over me.

'I can go no farther,' I said,
in a drowsy tone.
I became dogged and resolved.
I *would* sleep,
even if only for five minutes.
Even if death were to be the result,
I *would* sleep.

Gregory stood still.
He knew what the cold was doing to me.

dogged and resolved
– stupidly determined

Gregory speaks in a very gentle, old-fashioned, Northern accent. He uses 'thee' and 'thou' for 'you'.

Hast – have you

He felt it was cruel of Gregory to keep him awake.

Hie thee home – go home quickly

'It is of no use' said he, as if to himself.
'We are no nearer home
than we were when we started.
Our only chance is in Lassie.
Here! roll thee in my cloak, lad,
and lay thee down on the sheltered side
of this rock.
Creep close under it, lad,
and I'll lay by thee,
and try to keep the warmth in us.
Stay! Hast got anything about thee
they'll know at home?'

I felt him unkind to keep me from sleep,
but I pulled out my handkerchief
which aunt Fanny had sewn for me.
Gregory took it,
and tied it round Lassie's neck.

'Hie thee, Lassie, hie thee home!'
And she was off like a shot
in the darkness.

Now might I lie down –
Now might I sleep.
In my drowsiness I felt
that I was being tenderly covered up
by my brother,
but with what I neither knew nor cared –
I was too dull, too selfish,
too numb to think,
or I might have known
that in that bleak, bare place
there was nothing to wrap me in,
except what was taken off another.
I was glad enough when he had finished,
and lay down by me.

I took his hand.

'Thou canst not remember, lad,
how we lay together thus
by our dying mother.
She put thy small, wee hand in mine –
I reckon she sees us now;
and belike we shall soon be with her.
Anyhow, God's will be done.'

Think about this.
He is being wrapped
in a coat, but where
has that coat come
from?

belike – probably

'Dear Gregory,' I muttered,
and crept nearer to him for warmth.
He was talking still,
and again about our mother,
when I fell asleep.

In an instant – or so it seemed –
there were many voices about me –
many faces hovering round me.
The sweet luxury of warmth
was stealing into every part of me.
I was in my own little bed at home.

I am thankful to say,
my first word was 'Gregory?'

A look passed from one to another –
my father's stern old face tried in vain
to keep its sternness;

quivered – trembled

his mouth quivered,
his eyes slowly filled up with tears.

'I would have given him half my land –
I would have blessed him as my son –
oh God! I would have knelt at his feet,
and asked him to forgive
my hardness of heart.'

I heard no more.

consciousness –
he woke up

I came slowly to consciousness,
weeks afterwards.
My father's hair was white
when I recovered,
and his hand shook as he looked
into my face.

We spoke no more of Gregory.
We could not speak of him,
but he was strangely in our thoughts.
Lassie came and went.
My father would try to stroke her,
but she shrank away.

Aunt Fanny – always a talker –
told me all.
How on that fatal night,
my father, angry and worried,
had been fierce and sharp with Gregory,
even more than usual.
At last Gregory had risen up,
and whistled Lassie out with him.

Three hours afterwards,
when all were running about
in wild alarm,
not knowing where to go
in search of me –
not even missing Gregory, poor fellow –
poor, poor fellow! –
Lassie came home, with my handkerchief
tied round her neck.

They knew and understood,
and the whole farm was turned out
to follow her,
with wraps, and blankets, and brandy,
and everything that could be thought of.

I lay in chilly sleep, but still alive,
beneath the rock that Lassie
guided them to.
I was covered over
with my brother's cloak,
and his thick shepherd's coat
was carefully wrapped round my feet.

He was in his shirt-sleeves –
his arm thrown over me –
a quiet smile upon his still, cold face.

My father laid him in the same grave
as his mother.

He was soon to join them.

His last words were,
'God forgive me
for my hardness of heart
towards the fatherless child!'